MONSTERS OF THE ANIMAL KINGDOM

SCORPIONS

Rachel Lynette

PowerKiDS press

New York

For Adam

Published in 2013 by The Rosen Publishing Group, Inc.
29 East 21st Street, New York, NY 10010

First Edition

Editor: Jennifer Way
Book Design: Greg Tucker

Photo Credits: Cover Peter Bay/Shutterstock.com; p. 4 312010/Shutterstock.com; p. 4 James van den Broek/Shutterstock.com; p. 6 David Steele/Shutterstock.com; p. 7 (left) Craig K. Lorenz/Photo Researchers/Getty Images; pp. 7 (right), 16 Fletcher & Baylis/Photo Researchers/Getty Images; p. 8 Matthew Cole/Shutterstock.com; p. 9 Stana/Shutterstock.com; p. 10 Joao Paulo Burini/Flickr/Getty Images; p. 11 Gregory MD/Photo Researchers/Getty Images; pp. 12–13 Manamana/Shutterstock.com; pp. 14–15 Visuals Unlimited, Inc./Thomas Marent/Getty Images; p. 17 Wayne Lynch/All Canada Photos/Getty Images; p. 18 John Cancalosi/Peter Arnold/Getty Images; p. 19 © B Trapp/age fotostock; p. 20 Daniel Alvarez/Shutterstock.com; p. 21 (left) Tuttle Merlin/Photo Researchers/Getty Images; p. 21 (right) Tim Laman/National Geographic/Getty Images; p. 22 Braam Collins/Shutterstock.com.

Library of Congress Cataloging-in-Publication Data

Lynette, Rachel.
Scorpions / by Rachel Lynette. — 1st ed.
    p. cm. — (Monsters of the animal kingdom)
Includes index.
ISBN 978-1-4488-9633-2 (library binding) — ISBN 978-1-4488-9722-3 (pbk.) —
ISBN 978-1-4488-9727-8 (6-pack)
1. Scorpions—Juvenile literature. I. Title.
QL458.7.L96 2013
595.4'8—dc23

2012019920

Manufactured in the United States of America
CPSIA Compliance Information: Batch #W13PK5: For Further Information contact Rosen Publishing, New York, New York at 1-800-237-9932

CONTENTS

SCARY SCORPIONS

What has eight legs, two big claws, and a **venomous** stinging tail? It is a scorpion! Scorpions not only look scary, they can also be dangerous. There are around 30 **species** of scorpions that have venom that is strong enough to kill a human.

Scorpions are known for their large front claws and for their curved tails, which have stingers on the ends.

Spiders and scorpions belong to the same scientific class.

There are about 1,500 species of scorpions on Earth. They are related to other eight-legged animals, including spiders and ticks. Scorpions are some of the oldest animals on our planet. They have been around for over 400 million years. That means that there were scorpions roaming the earth even before the dinosaurs!

AT HOME IN THE GROUND

Scorpions can be found on every continent except Antarctica. Many people think of scorpions as desert animals, but that is not the only place they live. While most scorpions prefer warm climates, they can live in forests, grasslands, caves, and even in the mountains.

The Arabian scorpion, shown here, lives in the desert in the Middle East.

Left: The northern desert hairy scorpion is found in the southwestern United States. *Right*: Asian forest scorpions, like the one shown here, live in tropical forests in Southeast Asia.

About 90 species of scorpions live in the United States. Most of these species can be found in Arizona, New Mexico, Texas, and California.

Most species of scorpions live in burrows that they dig themselves in the sand or dirt. Scorpions also live between rocks, under rocks, and under leaves and bark.

DANGEROUS BODY

Most scorpions are about 2.5 inches (6 cm) long. That is about the size of an adult's thumb. A scorpion's body is formed into two sections that are made up of smaller **segments**. Along its body are eight legs. Scorpions do not have bones, as people do. Instead, a scorpion has a hard **exoskeleton**.

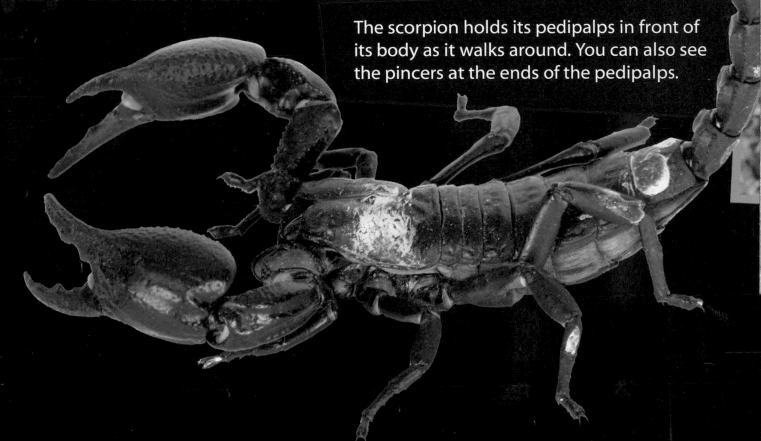

The scorpion holds its pedipalps in front of its body as it walks around. You can also see the pincers at the ends of the pedipalps.

The emperor scorpion, sh[own]
here, is one of the largest
scorpions in the world. It c[an grow]
up to 8 inches (20 cm) long[.]

At its front, a scorpion has a pair of large body parts called **pedipalps**. Each of the pedipalps has a large claw or pincer at the end. The pincers are used to capture **prey**, fight **predators**, and dig burrows.

DEADLY STINGER

A scorpion's stinger is at the end of its tail on a body part called the **telson**. There are two **glands** inside the telson that store the venom. When the scorpion squeezes these glands, the venom flows through the stinger.

One of the deadliest scorpions is the Indian red scorpion, which lives throughout India and Pakistan. The South African fat-tail scorpion can spray venom up to 3 feet (1 m). If it gets in a victim's eyes, the venom can cause blindness!

This close-up is of a scorpion's telson. The stinger is the curved part at the end.

The deathstalker scorpion lives in North Africa and the Middle East. It has such a fearsome name because its venom can seriously hurt or even kill a person.

SCARY FACTS

1 All scorpions glow a bright blue-green color if they are put under a special kind of light. Scientists think this feature helps the scorpion detect light.

2 Scorpions can control how much venom they release. They use a lot of venom for larger prey and less for smaller prey.

3 A mother scorpion will eat her own babies if there is no other food available!

4 Scorpions can slow their **metabolisms** so that they do not need much energy. A scorpion can slow its metabolism enough to live on just one insect a year.

5 Cave scorpions live in total darkness for their entire lives. They are blind because they do not have eyes.

6 Worldwide, about 3,250 people die from scorpion stings each year.

7 Scorpio is a scorpion-shaped constellation, or grouping of stars in the night sky.

8 In the video game *Deadly Creatures*, you can play as either a scorpion or a tarantula as you fight against lizards, wasps, and even humans.

13

GOING SOLO

Other than when they **mate**, most scorpions spend their lives alone. They are **nocturnal** and spend most of their time hiding alone in their burrows. If two scorpions do meet, one is likely to try to eat the other one.

One species of scorpion that does live with others of its kind is the bark scorpion. Bark scorpions sometimes burrow together in groups during the colder winter months. Bark scorpions live in California, Arizona, and New Mexico. Emperor scorpions also live together. They live in family groups and even work together when hunting. Emperor scorpions can be found in western Africa.

Most scorpions, like this one, will fight scorpions of their own species they meet unless it is mating season.

AMBUSH!

Scorpions eat mostly insects and spiders. Some larger species of scorpions prey on lizards, snakes, and rodents. Most scorpions do not look for food. Instead, they wait for food to come to them. When a scorpion senses that prey is nearby, it grabs it with its pincers. It will use its stinger only if the prey is very large or hard to

Here a cave scorpion has captured a cockroach for its dinner.

This northern scorpion is eating a blowfly in British Columbia, Canada.

hold. Next, the scorpion covers the prey with its own **digestive juices**. The juices turn the animal's insides into liquid. The scorpion sucks the liquid into its stomach, leaving the hard parts behind.

SCORPION BABIES

Scorpions mate in late spring through early fall. A mother scorpion gives birth to about 25 babies. Depending on the species, she will have babies anywhere from a few months to a year after mating.

The young scorplings shown here have not yet molted for the first time. For now, they are much safer up on their mother's back than on the ground.

When a male scorpion finds a female to mate with, he will grab her pedipalps and do a courtship "dance" before mating with her.

Newborn scorpions are soft and white. As soon as they are born, they crawl up onto their mother's back, where they may stay for up to 50 days. Scorpions leave their mother when they **molt** for the first time. Scorpions molt when they outgrow their old exoskeletons. Scorpions molt about five times before they are full grown.

SCORPIONS FOR SUPPER

You might think that scorpions do not have any predators, but that is not true. Many animals, including owls, bats, lizards, snakes, frogs, and rodents, eat scorpions. Scorpions also eat one another. In addition, people in China and parts of Africa eat scorpions.

A scorpion's tail is its best defense against predators. However, many predators attack by first breaking off

The meerkat, shown here, is one animal that is not harmed by scorpion venom. It lives in the Kalahari Desert and the Namib Desert, in Africa.

Left: The pallid bat is a North American bat that eats scorpions. Here, this bat is taking a scorpion back to its roost to eat it. *Below*: The southern ground hornbill, shown here, is an African bird that preys on scorpions.

the tail so they cannot be stung. Other predators can attack scorpions with no fear of being stung because they are not harmed by the scorpion's venom. These animals include meerkats and some kinds of snakes.

FRIEND OR FOE?

Most people do not like scorpions and may even kill them if they see them in the wild. Several species of scorpions are even endangered.

However, some people like scorpions and keep them as pets. People who keep pet scorpions must be very careful to take care of them safely. Scorpions can be useful to people, too. Scientists are finding ways to use scorpion venom as a painkiller and to help treat illnesses like cancer.

Careful owners may handle their pet scorpions, but some species cannot be handled safely.

GLOSSARY

digestive juices (dy-JES-tiv JOOS-ez) Matter in the body that helps break down food into energy.

exoskeleton (ek-soh-SKEH-leh-tun) The hard covering on the outside of an animal's body that holds and guards the soft insides.

glands (GLANDZ) Organs or parts of the body that produce elements to help with bodily functions.

mate (MAYT) To come together to make babies.

metabolisms (meh-TA-buh-lih-zumz) The speed at which bodies use energy.

molt (MOHLT) To shed hair, feathers, shell, horns, or skin.

nocturnal (nok-TUR-nul) Active during the night.

pedipalps (PEH-duh-palps) The second pair of legs on arachnids.

predators (PREH-duh-terz) Animals that kill other animals for food.

prey (PRAY) An animal that is hunted by another animal for food.

segments (SEG-ments) Single parts of something.

species (SPEE-sheez) One kind of living thing. All people are one species.

telson (TEL-sun) The rear part of certain animals, like the stinger of a scorpion.

venomous (VEH-nuh-mis) Having matter that can cause pain or death.

INDEX

WEBSITES

Due to the changing nature of Internet links, PowerKids Press has developed an online list of websites related to the subject of this book. This site is updated regularly. Please use this link to access the list: www.powerkidslinks.com/mak/scorp/